D0921144

Gallery Books
Editor: Peter Fallon

THE MIDNIGHT VERDICT

Seamus Heaney

THE MIDNIGHT VERDICT

Gallery Books

The Midnight Verdict
was first published
in December 1993
in a limited clothbound edition.
First paperback edition
November 2000.

The Gallery Press
Loughcrew
Oldcastle
County Meath
Ireland

ISBN 1 85235 282 5

'Orpheus and Eurydice' and 'The Death of Orpheus' appeared in *After Ovid*, edited by Michael Hofmann and James Lasdun, 1994.

The Gallery Press acknowledges the financial assistance of An Chomhairle Ealaíon / The Arts Council, Ireland, and the Arts Council of Northern Ireland.

THE MIDNIGHT VERDICT

for Jean and Peter

Translator's Note

The three translations included here were all part of a single impulse. 'Orpheus and Eurydice' was done in June 1993, just before I began to prepare a lecture on *Cúirt an Mheán Oíche* (1780) for the Merriman Summer School. Then, in order to get to closer grips with the original, I started to put bits of the Irish into couplets and, in doing so, gradually came to think of the Merriman poem in relation to the story of Orpheus, and in particular the story of his death as related by Ovid. The end of *The Midnight Court* took on a new resonance when read within the acoustic of the classical myth, and this gave me the idea of juxtaposing the Irish poem (however drastically abridged) with the relevant passages from Ovid's *Metamorphoses.*

Seamus Heaney

ORPHEUS AND EURYDICE

Ovid, Metamorphoses, *Book X*

Orpheus called for Hymen and Hymen came
Robed in saffron like a saffron flame
Leaping across tremendous airy zones
To reach the land of the Ciconians.
So Hymen did attend the rites, but no
Good luck or cheer or salutations, no
Auspicious outcome was to come of that.
Instead, the torch he carried smoked and spat
And no matter how he fanned it wouldn't flare.
His eyes kept watering. And a worse disaster
Than could have been predicted came to pass
For as the bride went roaming through the grass
With all her naiads round her, she fell down.
A snake had bit her ankle. She was gone.

Orpheus mourned her in the world above,
Raving and astray, until his love
Compelled him down among the very shades.
He dared to venture on the Stygian roads
Among those shadow people, the many, many
Ghosts of the dead, to find Persephone
And the lord who rules the dismal land of Hades;
Then plucked the lyre-gut for its melodies

And sang in harmony: 'O founded powers
Who rule the underearth, this life of ours,
This mortal life we live in upper air
Will be returned to you. To you, therefore,
We may speak the whole truth and speak it out
As I do now, directly: I have not
Transgressed your gloomy borders just to see
The sights of Tartarus, nor to tie all three
Of the three-necked monster's snake-snarled necks in one.
I crossed into your jurisdiction
Because my wife is here. The snake she stepped on
Poisoned her and cut her off too soon
And though I have tried to suffer on my own
And outlive loss, in the end Love won.
Whether or not you underpowers feel
The force of this god, Love, I cannot tell,
But surely he prevails down here as well
Unless that ancient story about hell
And its lord and a ravaged girl's not true.
Was it not Love that bound the two of you?
I pray you, therefore, by the extent of these
Scaresome voids and mist-veiled silences,
Unweave the woven fate Eurydice
Endured too soon. All of humanity
Is in your power, your kingdom is our home.
We may put off the day but it will come.
Sooner or later, the last house on the road
Will be this immemorial abode.
This is the throne-room of the universe.
Allow Eurydice her unlived years
And when she will have lived them, she'll be yours

Inalienably. I desire on sufferance
And want my wife. But if the fates pronounce
Against this privilege, then you can take
Credit for two deaths. I shall not go back.'

As Orpheus played and pleaded, the bodiless
Hordes of the dead wept for him. Tantalus
Was so bewitched he let the next wave fill
And fall without reaching. Ixion's wheel
Stood spellbound. The vultures' beaks held off
Above Tityos' liver. The obsessive
Water-riddlers heard and did not move.
And Sisyphus, you dozed upon your rock
Which stood dazed also. A tear then wet the cheek
Of each of the Eumenides, the one
And only time: song had made them human
And made the lord of Hades and his lady
Relent as well. They called Eurydice
Who limped out from among the newly dead
As eager as the day when she'd been wed
To Orpheus. But there was one term set:
Until he left Avernus, he was not
To look back, or the gift would be in vain.

They took the pathway up a steep incline
That kept on rising higher, through a grim
Silence and thick mist, and they had come
Close to the rim of earth when Orpheus —
Anxious for her, wild to see her face —
Turned his head to look and she was gone
Immediately, forever, back and down.

He reached his arms out, desperate to hold
And be held on to, but his arms just filled
With insubstantial air. She died again,
Bridal and doomed, but still did not complain
Against her husband — as indeed how could she
Complain about being loved so totally?
Instead, as she slipped away, she called out dear
And desperate farewells he strained to hear.

The second death stunned Orpheus. He stood
Disconsolate, beyond himself, dumbfounded
Like the man who turned to stone because he'd seen
Hercules lead Cerberus on a chain
Leashed to his middle neck; or like that pair
Petrified to two rocks underwater
In the riverlands of Ida — Olenos
And Lethea, uxorious sinners.
Pleading and pleading to be let across
The Styx again, he sat for seven days
Fasting and filthy on the bank, but Charon
Would not allow it. So he travelled on
Accusing the cruel gods until he found
A way back to his mountainous home ground
In Rhodope.

The sun passed through the house
Of Pisces three times then, and Orpheus
Withdrew and turned away from loving women —
Perhaps because there only could be one
Eurydice, or because the shock of loss
Had changed his very nature. Nonetheless,

Many women loved him and, denied
Or not, adored. But now the only bride
For Orpheus was going to be a boy
And Thracians learned from him, who still enjoy
Plucking those spring flowers bright and early.

THE MIDNIGHT VERDICT

Excerpted from Brian Merriman's Cúirt an Mheán Oíche;
lines 1-194 and an abridged version of lines 855-1026.

ONE

I used to wade through heavy dews
On the riverbank, in the grassy meadows,
Beside the woods, in a glen apart
As the morning light lit sky and heart
And sky and heart kept growing lighter
At the sight of Graney's clear lough water.
The lift of the mountains there! Their brows
Shining and stern in serried rows!
My withered heart would start to quicken,
Everything small in me, hardbitten,
Everything hurt and needy and shrewd
Lifted its eyes to the top of the wood
Past flocks of ducks on a glassy bay
And a swan there too in all her glory;
Jumping fish in the heady light
And the perch's belly flashing white.
The sheen of the lough, the grumble and roar
Of the blue-black waves as they rolled ashore.
There'd be chirruping birds from tree to tree
And leaping deer in the woods nearby,
Sounding of horns, the dashing crowd
As the hounds gave tongue and Reynard fled.

Yesterday morning the sky was clear,
The sun flamed up in the house of Cancer
With the night behind it, fit to take on
The work of the day that had to be done.
Leafy branches were all around me,
Shooting grasses and growths abounded;
There were green plants climbing and worts and weeds
That would gladden your mind and clear your head.
I was tired out, dead sleepy and slack,
So I lay at my length on the flat of my back
With my head well propped, my limbs at ease
In a nest in a ditch beside the trees.
The minute I closed my eyes, I drowsed.
My lids were locked, I couldn't be roused.
I was hidden from flies, felt safe and sound
When a nightmare swarmed and gathered around,
Battered me, flattened me, dragged me down
Through weltering sleep and left me stunned.
But my rest was short for next there comes
A sound from the ground like the roll of drums,
A wind from the north, a furious rout
And the lough in a sulphurous thunderlight.
And then comes looming into view
And steering towards me along the bay
This hefty menacing dangerwoman,
Bony and huge, a terrible hallion.
Her height, I'd say, to the nearest measure,
Was six or seven yards or more,
With a swatch of her shawl all muck and japs
Streeling behind in the puddly gaps.
It was awe-inspiring just to see her,
So hatchet-faced and scarred and sour —

With her ganting gums and her mouth in a twist
She'd have put the wind up man or beast.
And Lord of Fates! Her hand was a vise
Clamped on a towering staff or mace
With a spike on top and a flange of brass
That indicated her bailiff's powers.

Her words were grim when she got started.
'Get up,' she said, 'and on your feet!
What do you think gives you the right
To shun the crowds and the sitting court?
A court of justice, truly founded,
And not the usual rigged charade,
But a fair and clement court of women
Of the gentlest stock and regimen.
The Irish race should be grateful always
For a bench that's so composed and wise
And in session now, two days and a night,
In the spacious fort on Graney Height.

Their king, moreover, has taken to heart
The state of the country; he feels its hurt
As if it were his own, and the whole
Of his entourage are aghast as well.
It's goodbye to freedom and ancient right,
To honest dealing and leadership:
The ground ripped off and nothing put back,
Weeds in the field once crop is stacked.
With the best of the people leaving the land,
Graft has the under- and upper hand.
Just line your pockets, a wink and a nod,
And to hell with the poor! Their backs are broad.

Alas for the plight of the underclass
And the system's victims who seek redress:
Their one recourse is the licensed robber
With his legalese and his fancy slabber.
Lawyers corrupt, their standards gone,
Favouritism the way it's done,
The bar disgraced, truth compromised,
Nothing but kick-backs, bribes and lies.

To add to which, the whole assembly
Decreed on the Bible this very day:
The youth has failed, declined, gone fallow —
Bad news and bad marks, sir, for you.
In living memory, with birth rates fallen
And marriage in Ireland on the wane,
The country's life has been dissipated,
Pillage and death have combined to waste it.
Blame arrogant kings, blame emigration,
But it's you and your spunkless generation.
You're a source blocked off that won't refill.
You have failed your women, one and all.

Think of the way they're made and moulded,
The flush and zest in their flesh and blood —
Those easy ladies half on offer
And the big strait-laced ones, all ignored.
Why aren't they all consoled and gravid,
In full proud sail with their breasts in bud?
Say but the word and the clustered fruit
Will be piled like windfalls round your feet.

So the meeting pondered the country's crisis
And the best opinions agreed on this:
That one of their own should be deputed
To come back here to adjudicate.
Then Aoibheall rises, as Munster's guardian
And Craglee's peerless fairy queen
And offers to leave the fairy palace
And go to Thomond to hear the case.
And, honest princess, she makes a promise
To come down hard on the law's abuse.
Might without right to be defeated
And right as right reinstated straight.
So hereinafter, greasing the palm
Of pimp or madam or sycophant
Won't work or avail, for it's not an inch
Now that Her Grace is boss of the bench.
Already at Feakle the court's in session
That you must answer. The pressure's on
For you to appear. So move. And fast.
Move or I'll make you move, you bast- .'

With that she crooked her staff in my cape
And hooked me behind and hauled me up
And we went like hell over glen and hill
To Moinmoy Church, by the gable wall.

And there (I am sure) lit torches showed
A handsome, grand, well-built abode,
A stately, steadfast, glittering space,
Accessible and commodious.
And I saw a lovely vision woman
Ensconced on the bench of law and freedom,

And saw her fierce, fleet guard of honour
Rank upon rank in throngs around her.
I saw then too rooms filling full,
Crowding with women from wall to wall,
And saw this other heavenly beauty
With her lazy eye, on her dignity,
Seductive, pouting, with curling locks,
Biding her time in the witness box.
Her hair spilled down, loosed tress on tress,
And a hurt expression marked her face;
She was full of fight, with a glinting eye,
Hot on the boil, ill-set and angry —
Yet for all her spasms, she couldn't speak
For her hefts and huffing had made her weak.
She looked like death or a living death wish
She was so cried out; but straight as a rush,
She stood to the fore as a witness stands
Flailing and wailing and wringing hands.
And she kept it up; she raved and screeched
Till sighing restored her powers of speech.
Then her downlook went, her colour rose,
She dried her eyes and commenced as follows:

'A thousand welcomes! And bless Your Highness!
Aoibheall of Crag, our prophetess!
Our daylight's light, our moon forever,
Our hope of life when the weeping's over!
O head of all the hosted sisters,
Thomond can thole no more! Assist us!
My cause, my case, the reason why
My plea's prolonged so endlessly

Until I'm raving and round the twist
Like a maenad whirled in a swirl of mist —
The reason why is the unattached
And unprovided for, unmatched
Women I know, like flowers in a bed
Nobody's dibbled or mulched or weeded
Or trimmed or watered or ever tended;
So here they are, unhusbanded,
Unasked, untouched, beyond conception —
And, needless to say, I'm no exception.
I'm scorched and tossed, a sorry case
Of nerves and drives and neediness,
Depressed, obsessed, awake at night,
Unused, unsoothed, disconsolate,
A throbbing ache, a dumb discord,
My mind and bed like a kneading board.
O Warden of the Crag, incline!
Observe the plight of Ireland's women,
For if things go on like this, then fuck it!
The men will have to be abducted!'

TWO

Bathed in an aura of morning light,
Her Grace on the bench got up to her feet;
Beautiful, youthful, full of poise,
She cleared her throat and raised her voice,
Then clenched her fists with definite menace
And ordered the bailiff to call for silence.
The court complied; they sat entranced
As her lovely fluent lips pronounced:

'To my mind, girl, you've stated your case
With point and force. You deserve redress.
So I here enact a law for women:
Unmated men turned twenty-one
To be sought, pursued, and hunted down,
Tied to this tree beside the headstone,
Their vests stripped off, their jackets ripped,
Their backs and asses scourged and whipped.
But the long-in-the-tooth and the dry-in-marrow,
The ones whose harrow-pins won't harrow,
Who pen the pent and lock away
The ram that's rampant in their body,
Keeping in hand what should go the rounds
And fencing off the pleasure grounds —
Their nemesis I leave to you
Whose hearths they'd neither fan nor blow.
Dear natural sexual women, think!
Consult your gender, mind and instinct.

Take cognizance. Co-operate.
For I here invest you with the right
(To be exercised to the breaking point)
And powers of violent punishment.

Yet who gives a damn in the end of all
For them and their dribbling stroup and fall?
With forks collapsed and the feeling gone,
Their hardest part is a pubic bone.
So let them connive, sing dumb and smile
If ever a young man rings their bell
For it seems to me that the best solution
For men past making a contribution
Is not to resent their conjugal plight
But stand by their wives when they put it about,
Facilitate their womanly drives
And lend their name when the baby arrives.
And that, for the moment, will have to do.
I'm on the circuit, and overdue
In another part of Munster. So:
My verdict's short because I go.
But I'll be back, and God help then
Recalcitrant, male-bonded men.'

She stopped, but still her starry gaze
Transfixed me in a kind of daze
I couldn't shake off. My head went light,
I suffered cramps and a fainting fit.
The whole earth seemed to tilt and swing,
My two ears sang from the tongue-lashing
And then the awful targe who'd brought me,
The plank-armed bailiff, reached and caught me

Up by the ears and scruff of the neck
And dragged me struggling into the dock.
Where next comes skipping, clapping hands,
The lass who had aired her love-demands
And says to my face, 'You hardened chaw,
I've waited long, now I'll curry you raw!
You've had your warnings, you cold-rifed blirt.
But now you're caught in a woman's court
And nobody's here to plead your case.
Where is the credit you've earned with us?
Is there anyone here your action's eased?
One that your input's roused or pleased?
Observe him closely, Madam Judge.
From head to toe, he's your average
Passable male — no paragon
But nothing a woman wouldn't take on.
Unshapely, yes, and off the plumb,
But with all his kit of tools about him.
A shade whey-faced and pale and wan,
But what about it? There's bone and brawn.
For it's him and his likes with their humps and stoops
Can shoulder doors and flutter the coops;
As long as a man is randy and game,
Who gives a damn if he's bandy or lame?
So why is he single? Some secret wound
Or problem back in the family background?
And him the quality's darling boy,
All smiles and friends with everybody,
Playing his tunes, on sprees and batters
With his intellectual and social betters.
Wining and dining, day in, day out —
The creep, I can see why they think he's great!

A star bucklepper, the very man
You'd be apt to nickname 'merry man',
But the kind of man I would sweep away,
The virgin merry, going grey.
It bothers me deeply. I've come to hate
His plausible, capable, charming note
And his beaming, bland, unfurrowed forehead:
Thirty years old, and never bedded.

So hear me now, long-suffering judge!
My own long hurt and ingrown grudge
Have me desolated. I hereby claim
A woman's right to punish him.
And you, dear women, you must assist.
So rope him, Una, and all the rest —
Anna, Maura — take hold and bind him.
Double twist his arms behind him.
Remember all the sentence called for
And execute it to the letter.
Maeve and Sive and Sheila! Maureen!
Knot the rope till it tears the skin.
Let Mr Brian take what we give,
Let him have it. Flay him alive
And don't draw back when you're drawing blood.
Test all of your whips against his manhood.
Cut deep. No mercy. Make him squeal.
Leave him in strips from head to heel
Until every single mother's son
In the land of Ireland learns the lesson.

And it only seems both right and fitting
To note the date of this special sitting

So calm your nerves and start computing:
A thousand minus a hundred and ten —
Take what that gives you, double it, then
Your product's the year.' She'd lifted her pen
And her hand was poised to ratify
The fate that was looking me straight in the eye.
She was writing it down, the household guard
Sat at attention, staring hard
As I stared back. Then my dreaming ceased
And I started up, awake, released.

THE DEATH OF ORPHEUS

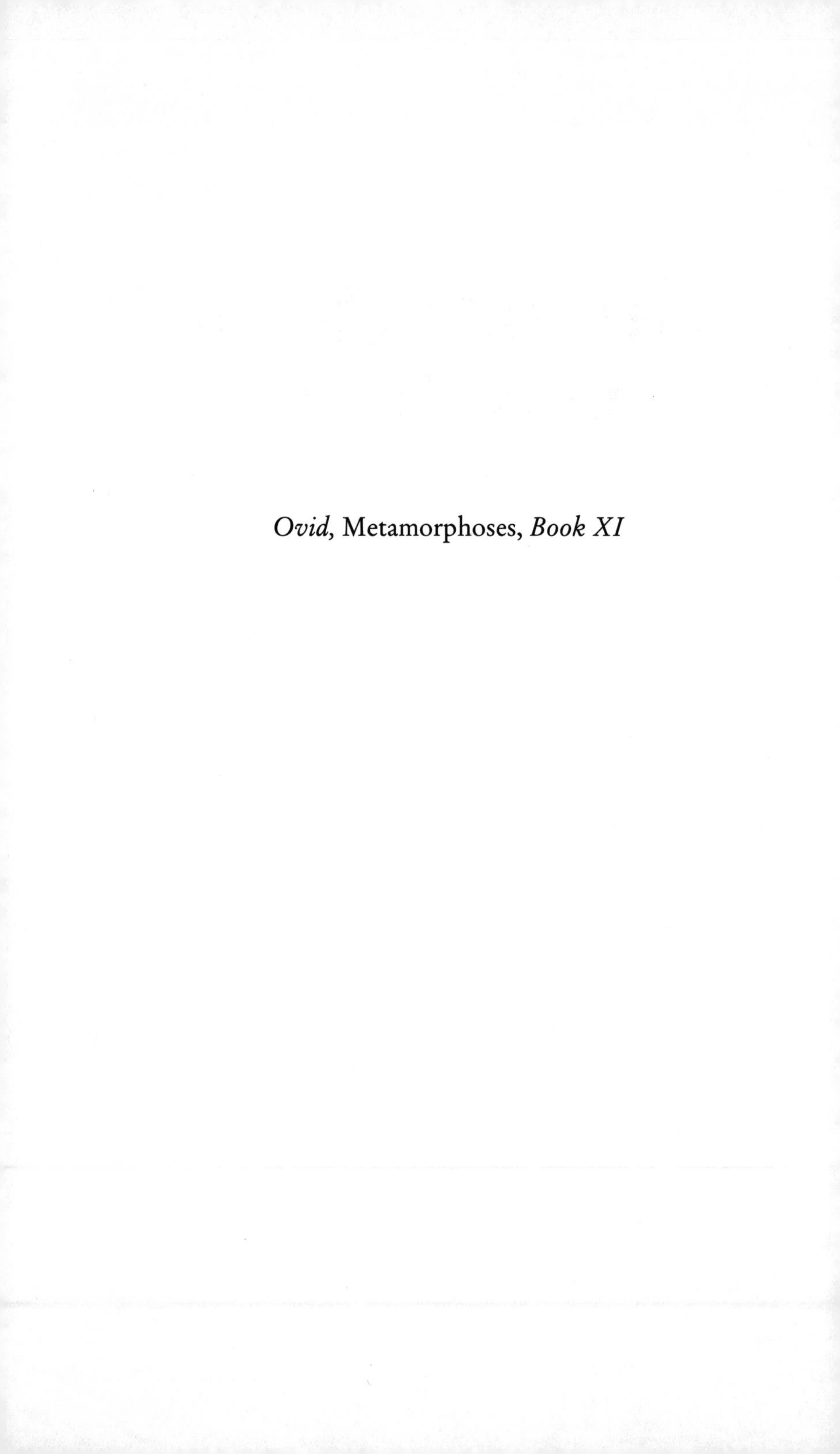

Ovid, Metamorphoses, *Book XI*

The songs of Orpheus held the woods entranced.
The animals were hushed, the field-stones danced
Until a band of crazed Ciconian women,
A maenad band dressed up in wild beasts' skins,
Spied him from a hilltop with his lyre.
As he tuned his voice to it and cocked his ear,
One of them whose hair streamed in the breeze
Began to shout, 'Look, look, it's Orpheus,
Orpheus the misogynist,' and flung
Her staff straight at the bard's mouth while he sang.
But the staff being twined with leaves just left a bruise
And did no injury. So another throws
A stone that his singing spellbinds in the air,
Making it drop like a shamed petitioner
At his affronted feet. But even so,
There could be no stop to the violence now.
The furies were unleashed. And his magic note
That should have stalled their weapons was drowned out
By blaring horns and drums, beatings and yells
And the pandemonium of those bacchanals
So that at last his red blood wet the rocks.
But first the maenads ripped apart the snakes

And the flocks of birds he'd charmed out of the sky
And the dreambound beasts that formed his retinue.
Orpheus then, torn by their blood-filled nails,
Was like an owl in daytime when it falls
Prey to the hawks of light; or a stag that stands
In the amphitheatre early, before the hounds
Have savaged it to pieces on the sand.
They circled him, still using as their weapons
Staffs they had twined with leaves and tipped with cones
That were never meant for duty such as this.
Some pelted him with clods, some stripped the branches
To scourge him raw, some stoned him with flintstones.
But as their frenzy peaked, they chanced upon
Far deadlier implements.

Near at hand
Oxen in yokes pulled ploughshares through the ground
And sturdy farmers sweated as they dug —
Only to flee across their drills and rigs
When they saw the horde advancing. They downed tools
So there for the taking on the empty fields
Lay hoes and heavy mattocks and long spades.
The oxen lowered their horns, the squealing maenads
Cut them to pieces, then turned to rend the bard,
Committing sacrilege when they ignored
His hands stretched out to plead and the extreme
Pitch of his song that now for the first time
Failed to enchant. And so, alas, the breath
Of life streamed out of him, out of that mouth
Whose songs had tamed the beasts and made stones dance,
And was blown away on the indiscriminate winds.

For Orpheus then the birds in cheeping flocks,
The animals in packs, the flint-veined rocks
And woods that had listened, straining every leaf,
Wept and kept weeping. For it seemed as if
The trees were mourners tearing at their hair
As the leaves streamed off them and the branch went bare.
And rivers too, they say, rose up in floods
Of their own tears, and all the nymphs and naiads
Went dishevelled in drab mourning gowns.
Meanwhile, the poet's mangled flesh and bones
Lay scattered and exposed. But his head and lyre
Were saved by miracle: the Hebrus River
Rose for them, ran with them, bore them out midstream
Where the lyre trembled and the dead mouth swam
Lapping the ripples that lipped the muddy shore
And a fluent humming sadness filled the air.
As they rode the current downstream, they were swept
On out to sea off Lesbos and washed up
On the strand there, unprotected. Then a snake
Unleashed itself like a slick whip to attack
The head in its tangled web of sopping locks
But Phoebus intervened. Just as its bite
Gaped at its widest, it solidified.
The jaws' hinge hardened and the open yawn
Of the empty vicious mouth was set in stone.

The poet's shade fled underneath the earth
Past landmarks that he recognized, down paths
He'd travelled on the first time, desperately
Scouring the blessed fields for Eurydice.
And when he found her, wound her in his arms
And moved with her, and she with him, two forms

Of the one love, restored and mutual —
For Orpheus now walks free, is free to fall
Out of step, into step, follow, go in front
And look behind him to his heart's content.

But Bacchus was unwilling to forget
The atrocities against his sacred poet,
So, there and then, in a web of roots, he wound
And bound the offending women to the ground.
However deftly they would try to go,
Earth's grip and traction clutched them from below.
They felt it latch them, load them heel and toe.
And, as a caught bird struggles to get free
From a cunningly set snare, but still can only
Tighten the mesh around its feet still tighter
The more it strains its wings and frets and flutters,
So each of the landlogged women heaved and hauled
In vain, in agony, as the roots took hold
And bark began to thicken the smooth skin.
It gripped them and crept up above their knees.
They struggled like a storm in storm-tossed trees.
Then, as each finger twigged and toe dug in,
Arms turned to oak boughs, thighs to oak, oak leaves
Matted their breasts and camouflaged their moves
So that you couldn't tell if the whole strange growth
Were a wood or women in distress or both.